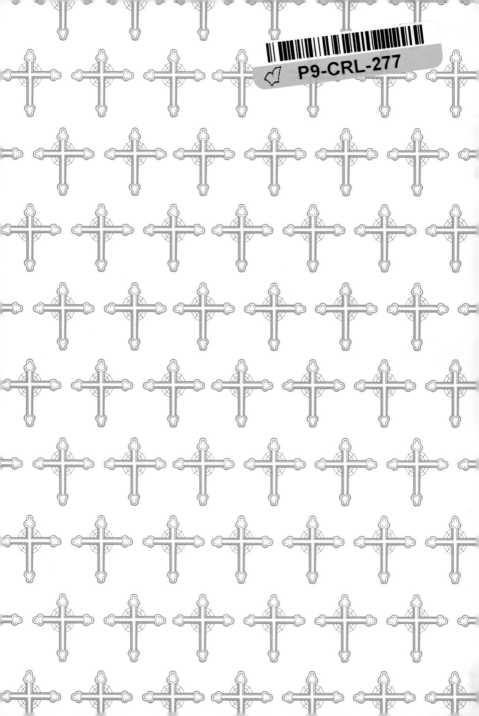

SAINTS FOR BOYS "HEROES OF GOD"

BY

DANIEL A. LORD, S.J.

1946 EDITION

NIHIL OBSTAT
JOHN M. FEARNS, S.T.D.

IMPRIMATUR
+ FRANCIS CARDINAL SPELLMAN, *Archbishop, New York*

CUM PERMISSU SUPERIORUM

Manufactured in Hong Kong through InterPress Ltd. - December 2012 --- Job# 121027

St. Aloysius Gonzaga

THE LITTLE JESUIT

Aloysius was the son of a very famous and noble family.

They expected him to make a name for himself in the world.

Instead, he promised God he would never marry. He asked to love God and Our Lady alone.

When he was very young, he became a Jesuit. From the very start, he was as holy as he could be. He kept his soul as pure as the whitest snow.

He loved Mary with all his heart. He stayed for hours on his knees before Christ in the Blessed Sacrament.

But he was a brave young man. When a terrible sickness came over the city, Aloysius went out to care for the sick. Once he brought home a very sick old man and nursed him in his own bed.

He wanted very much to be a priest.

But God wanted to show young people that even the very young can be saints. So he took Aloysius early with him to Heaven.

He is the special patron of boys and girls.

Boys and girls can all study as hard as he did. They can love Christ and Mary with all their hearts.

But most of all, they can be very pure.

His Feast is June 21st.

St. Andrew
THE FISHERMAN

Andrew was just a poor fisherman in Galilee. He had a brother whose name was Simon Peter.

One day he heard a great preacher, John the Baptist. He left his boats and fishing nets, and followed John.

And John said, "Someone is coming who is greater than I."

So when Jesus came, Andrew left John to follow Jesus. He ran and told Simon Peter. Peter went to Jesus too. Andrew and Peter both became Apostles.

Andrew was the Apostle who found the little boy with the loaves and fishes. Our dear Lord used these to feed thousands of people. That was a great miracle.

Jesus made Andrew one of His first Bishops.

"Go, teach everyone the Good News," Jesus said.

So after the Ascension of our Lord into heaven, Andrew went to Greece.

Some listened and became Christians.

But some hated Andrew because they hated Jesus.

So they nailed Andrew to a Cross. Andrew sang with joy because, like Jesus, he could die on the Cross.

He hung for two days on the Cross telling everyone about Jesus.

Then he went gloriously to heaven.

His Feast is November 30th.

St. Anthony
THE MIRACLE WORKER

When Anthony of Padua died, the children cried in the streets.

"Our dear father, Anthony is dead," they wept.

And all the bells of the churches rang of their own accord. Angels came to earth to ring the bells for the death of the saint.

Anthony wanted to be a martyr. He wanted to die for the love of Christ.

Instead, Our Lord asked him to work among the poor and needy.

So Anthony went about Italy working wonderful miracles for the people. He gave them miraculous food. He healed their sicknesses.

Whenever he spoke of Jesus, everyone listened and loved the Savior, too.

One night the Divine Child came to visit Anthony. He kissed the saint gently and told him how much He loved him. You have often seen statues of Saint Anthony with the Child in his arms.

Ever since his death, he has done wonderful things for those who pray to him. He is still the Franciscan Miracle-worker.

His Feast is June 13th.

St. Benedict

FATHER OF HOLY MONKS

The name Benedict means Blessed.

When Benedict was a boy, he realized that he was living in sad, not blessed days.

The world was full of savage and evil men. They made war on everybody. They destroyed beautiful buildings and burned wise books. They thought it was amusing to be destructive. They were very cruel.

Even the schoolboys were wicked and mean. They laughed at Benedict because he tried to be good.

So he ran away from the evil men and the sinful boys. He hid himself in a mountain near Subiaco.

He prayed. He studied. He talked with God. He asked God to make cruel men gentle and wicked little boys pure.

Soon many people heard about this wonderful young man. They hated war and evil men. So they ran up to the mountain and said to Benedict, "Let us stay with you."

Benedict built beautiful houses which are called monasteries. He dressed the good men as monks.

His sister, Saint Scholastica, dressed the women as nuns or sisters. She built convents.

In these the men and women prayed. They studied. They loved peace. They asked God to forgive sinners.

These men and women were the first Benedictines.

His Feast is July 11th.

St. Bernard

LEADER OF CHRISTIAN SOLDIERS

When Bernard went to be a monk and a priest, thirty of his young friends went with him.

Later on, his father became a priest. And all his brothers joined him in his monastery. He had only one sister. At first she was very gay and vain. But soon she became a nun, too.

That all showed how people loved Bernard and followed him.

He built a great monastery in a valley called Clairvaux. It was so strict people said, "No one will join." Instead, hundreds of brave young men came.

The Turks, who hated Christians, were very strong and had great armies. Bernard taught soldiers how to be fine pure knights. They became the Knights of the Temple.

He led the Christian armies to fight against the Turks. He carried only a crucifix.

But most of all, he loved Christ and Our Lady. As a boy, as a great priest, even in the army, he wrote beautiful songs to them. Some of them we sing to this day.

His Feast is August 20th.

St. Charles
LEADER OF PRIESTS

Charles Borromeo was a rich Italian young man. His family was noble. His uncle was Pope Pius IV.

But more than anything, Charles wanted to be a good priest.

At that time the Protestant churches had just begun. They did not believe in the Mass or the Blessed Sacrament.

Besides, because of war and disease, Italy badly needed good priests and fine Catholics.

So Charles became a priest. The Pope made him a Bishop very young. At once he worked hard for the poor. He took care of the sick in their own homes. When he preached, thousands came to hear him.

But often he sat by the road and taught one poor man his prayers.

He loved the Church because Christ loved it. He brought thousands back to Mass and Holy Communion. He built fine seminaries for priests, and schools for children.

In the end, a terrible sickness came to Milan, his city. Charles nursed the sick himself. He laid them on his own bed.

He died of the sickness, a martyr of charity.

His Feast is November 4th.

St. Christopher

THE CHRIST BEARER

Saint Christopher was a giant and very strong. He was a very brave soldier. "I will serve only the strongest men in the world," he said. So he fought in the army of a great, strong king.

But one day the soldier saw the king tremble and grow pale. The king was afraid of Satan. The thought of the Devil frightened him.

So Christopher, whose name was then Offero, went to serve the Devil. But soon he found that the Devil was afraid of someone too. Oh, he was very strong, but he was afraid of Jesus Christ.

"I will serve Jesus Christ," said Christopher.

So he went to a river where many travellers came. He carried them across on his strong shoulders. Some day, he thought, Jesus Christ might come that way.

Then one day a little Boy came to the river.

Christopher hoisted the Boy on his shoulders. He was very light. But as they crossed the river, He got heavier and heavier. "Who are You?" asked the giant. "I am Jesus Christ," said the Boy. "You looked for Me."

The giant was very happy. He became a Christian. His name became Christopher; that means, the man who carried Christ.

He is the patron saint of travellers. Especially he is the patron of those who travel in automobiles.

His traditional Feast is July 25th.

St. Dominic
THE GREAT PREACHER

Dominic was a fine, brave young Spaniard.

He was a smart student, too. He also loved the poor, and sold even his clothes and books to give money to those who were hungry.

In those days, evil men hated Jesus Christ and the truth. They were called Albigenses. They destroyed homes. They burned churches. They killed Catholics, especially priests and nuns.

Bravely Dominic decided to gather an army to fight them. Only his was an army of peace. He gathered fine young men and dressed them in white.

"I shall call you the Order of Preachers," he said. Nowadays we call these fine priests the Dominicans.

Dominic and his priests went everywhere and taught people the truth about Jesus Christ and goodness.

He gathered pure young women and dressed them in white too.

"You will pray for sinners," he said. These were the first Dominican nuns.

To help him win his battle of peace, Mary, our Blessed Mother, gave him a powerful weapon.

It was her Rosary. With that, Dominic and his brave men and pure women overcame the enemies of Christ and His Church.

His traditional Feast is August 4th.

St. Francis Of Assisi
THE PEACE SAINT

Many people say that St. Francis was the man who was most like Our Lord.

He saw how money makes many people bad and proud. So he wanted to be as poor as Our Lord was. He used to say, "I am married to Lady Poverty."

Far in the East are men called Moslems. They do not believe in Jesus Christ. So Francis went to visit them. And though they hated other Christians, they listened to Francis. They thought Jesus must be very fine, because Francis, His friend, was so good.

Once when Francis was praying a wonderful thing happened. God placed in his hands and feet the same marks that Our Lord carried after He was crucified. These are called Stigmata.

Francis preached about Jesus and Mary everywhere.

He built the first Christmas crib.

But so that everyone could hear about Our dear Lord, he gathered men and women to work with him. They worked among the poor people. They taught them how happy it is to be good.

They are called the Franciscans.

His Feast is October 4th.

St. Francis Xavier
THE MISSIONARY

Saint Francis Xavier went to the University of Paris. He was a champion runner. He was a great athlete.

But he was a very clever student, too.

In class, he was the leader. He learned easily. He studied hard.

"I want to be a great professor," he said. "I want to know all there is to know. I want people to listen when I talk. I want to write wonderful books."

Then he met Saint Ignatius Loyola.

"What good will it do you," Ignatius asked him, "if you win the whole world and then lose your soul?"

Francis thought this over. He decided he could win the world and at the same time save his soul. So he became a friend of Saint Ignatius. He became a Jesuit.

"Send me out," he said, "and I will win the world for our dear Lord."

So Ignatius sent him out as a missionary.

He went to India. He told people there about Jesus.

He went to Japan. The pagans listened. Many of them too became Catholics.

Then he wanted to go to China. Instead, he died on a little island just off the coast of China.

But he had converted thousands and thousands.

He was the greatest missionary since the days of the Apostles.

His Feast is December 3rd.

St. George

GREAT SOLDIER AND MARTYR

George was a strong and brave soldier in the army of the Roman Emperor Diocletian. Because of his courage, he quickly became one of the Emperor's favorite soldiers and Diocletian made him a colonel in the army.

Diocletian was an evil leader and hated all Christians and ordered them to be put to death.

But George was a Christian and stood up against the Emperor's command. Even though he knew that he might lose everything he had gained in his rank as a colonel in the army, he went to the Emperor and told him that he was wrong to put the Christians to death.

George was cast into prison because he was a Christian and he was put on trial for his religious beliefs. George would not back down even though the Emperor had him tortured. Diocletian finally had George led through the city and killed. Because he died for his Faith, we call him a martyr.

Pictures show George riding on a horse killing a dragon which is the symbol for evil or the devil. He was a soldier for Christ who stood up and fought against a very evil ruler. He is the patron saint of soldiers.

His Feast Day is April 23rd.

St. Gregory
THE GREAT POPE

Young Gregory's father was very rich.

When his father died, Gregory gave all the money he inherited to the poor. Then he went to a monastery and became a monk. He prayed. He studied hard.

The Pope of those days heard about this bright young man. He called Gregory to Rome. He made him a Deacon. He sent him on important errands to kings and generals.

One day in the market place, Gregory saw some slaves. They told him they were Angles.

"You should be Angels," he said.

English boys were called Angles in those days. Gregory knew they did not believe in Jesus. You see, he hoped they would be Catholics. When the Pope died, the people made Gregory the Pope.

He remembered the English boys. So he sent Saint Augustine to England to tell them about Jesus and to make them Catholics. He sent holy priests to convert the Spanish and the French. Wicked men came rushing into Italy to destroy it.

He told them about Jesus, and they became Catholics too. He wrote great books which are still read.

He taught people how to sing in Church. We still call these songs the Gregorian Chants.

He was one of the greatest Popes that ever lived.

His traditional Feast is March 12th.

St. Henry
EMPEROR

When Duke Henry of Bavaria was very young, he had a dream. His patron saint appeared to him and showed him the words, "After six."

The young man thought this meant he would die after six years. So he prepared for death. He lived like a saint.

Instead, after six years, he was chosen German emperor. But because for six years he had lived like a saint, he was a holy and great emperor.

He determined to rule for the glory of God and the good of his people. First he helped convert to Christ the nations near him who did not believe in the Savior.

A wicked man had driven the Pope from Rome. He was sitting on the Pope's own chair. Henry led his army against this bad man, beat him, and brought the Holy Father back to Rome.

Whenever he entered the city, his first visit was always to Christ in the Blessed Sacrament. Once Christ rewarded him wonderfully. Henry saw Jesus Himself say Mass in a great church in Rome.

Both Henry and his wife, Cunegunda, became great saints.

His traditional Feast is July 15th.

St. James

THE GREATER

James was one of the three Apostles Jesus kept nearest to Him.

The other two were Peter and John.

Like so many of the Apostles, James was a fisherman.

He followed Our Lord up the mountain when His face became bright as the Sun.

He was in the room when Jesus brought the little dead girl back to life.

When our dear Lord suffered the Agony in the Garden, James was near Him.

He had a fierce temper which he conquered with difficulty. But he had great faith and preached powerfully. So he was called the Son of Thunder.

After Our Lord ascended into Heaven, James bravely went around telling everyone about the Savior.

King Herod was angry. He cried, "Do you believe in Jesus Christ?"

"Indeed I do," James answered at once.

So the soldiers cut off his head with a sword, and he died a martyr.

His Feast is July 25th.

St. John
THE BELOVED APOSTLE

John was a young fisherman in the Holy Land.

One day, our dear Lord said to him, "Come and follow Me." Quickly he left family, boat, everything, and became an Apostle.

He saw Our Lord heal the sick and raise the dead. He heard the wonderful things Our Lord taught. He loved Jesus very much.

He sat next to Jesus the night when He gave His Apostles their First Communion.

Then when the other Apostles ran away from Calvary, John stayed on beside Mary. And Jesus gave this young man Mary for his Mother.

He became a great bishop. He wrote the Fourth Gospel and beautiful letters.

He took care of Mary after Jesus ascended into Heaven.

The Romans tried to kill him by boiling him in oil. But Jesus protected him. He was not even hurt.

Because he was very pure, Jesus loved him best of all the Apostles.

His Feast is December 27th.

St. Joseph

FOSTER FATHER OF JESUS

Joseph was a poor carpenter of Nazareth.

Yet he came from the royal family of David. And he was pure and good and hard working.

God knew He could trust Joseph, so He chose him for a most important task. He became the husband of Mary and the Foster Father of Our Lord.

So he protected Mary on the way to Bethlehem. He was present on the first Christmas. He led Mary and Jesus safely into Egypt when Herod was trying to kill the Child.

Later he worked for them. He made them a sweet little home. He earned money to give them their food and clothing.

When Jesus was a big boy, Joseph taught Him the carpenter's trade.

Joseph did not live to see Jesus become great and famous. Instead he died happily with Mary at his bedside, and Jesus blessing him.

He worked very hard to make life safe and happy for Jesus and Mary.

So Jesus has made him the Protector of the Whole Church.

His Feast is March 19th.

St. Jude

SAINT OF THE HOPELESS

Saint Jude is also called Saint Jude Thaddeus. He had three brothers. Their names were Saint James the Less, Saint Simeon of Jerusalem, and Joseph. Saint Jude and his three brothers were brethren of Jesus.

Saint Jude Thaddeus was one of the twelve apostles of Jesus. His kinship to our Saviour filled him with joy. He had the ardor of holy zeal and love. He was ready to sacrifice and to suffer for the Master's sake. He wanted to tell all the people the truth about Jesus.

After the Lord ascended into Heaven, Saint Jude set out with his companions to preach the Gospel. With only the word of God and his spirit he won out over evil.

Everywhere he went people listened to him. He traveled far, in Judaea, in Samaria, in Syria and in Mesopotamia. In his travels he met Saint Simeon and they preached together.

Everywhere he went he taught people to be humble. He taught them to be meek. He taught them to pray. He taught them to love God.

He said, "We owe God praise and thanks for His endless mercy." Saint Jude wrote a long letter. This letter was to all the Jewish converts, among whom he preached. The letter is called "The Epistle to the Hebrew Christians."

Saint Jude chose to suffer rather than give up his faith. While he was in Mesopotamia he converted many sinners. His enemies put him to death. He suffered martyrdom.

Saint Jude is regarded as the special patron of the sick, especially those whose cases seem to be helpless.

His Feast is October 28th.

St. Lawrence
THE DEACON

Lawrence was a fine young Roman.

He was chosen a deacon. That meant that it was his work to care for the sick and the poor.

But the Romans thought he was the treasurer of the Church.

So they took him prisoner. "Show us the treasures of the Church," they cried.

Lawrence had a great sense of humor.

"Gladly," he answered.

The Romans hurried after him, expecting to find gold and precious stones. Instead, he led them to the hospital where the poor and the sick lived.

"Here are the treasures of the Church," he cried. They were furious. But Lawrence knew how God loves the poor and needy.

In the end, the Romans put him to death. They laid him on a gridiron over a fire. But even there, Lawrence could joke.

"Turn me over," he cried, as the fire burned, "for I think I am done on this side."

Even in his pain, God gave Lawrence deep happiness.

His Feast is August 10th.

St. Leo
THE GREAT POPE

The name Leo means the Lion.

And Saint Leo, the Pope, was a lion in bravery.

The Vandals and Huns, two terrible races, were fighting the Christians of Europe.

Besides this, evil men were teaching people lies about Jesus. They were saying what was not true and getting the people confused. Leo became Pope. He had been a smart and wise young man.

Now he had to be a brave and very wise Pope.

First he went everywhere teaching the truth about our dear Lord. He called together all the wise priests and bishops of the Church. This was the great Council of Chalcedon.

They talked and studied and listened.

And they went home to teach their people the truth. So people did not believe the evil men any more when they lied about the Savior.

But the Vandals and Huns kept coming. They burned cities. They murdered people everywhere.

All alone, without weapons, Leo went out to meet them.

Their leader Attila was called the Awful Scourge.

But when he saw Leo he ordered his armies to cease fighting. Instead of destroying Rome, they turned and went away. The Pope had saved Europe.

His traditional Feast is April 11th.

St. Luke The Evangelist

THE ARTIST

Saint Luke studied medicine when he was a young man and became a great doctor.

He was also a skillful painter.

One day he heard about Jesus Christ. He knew that Jesus was the Great Physician. He was sure that Jesus was the God who had made all the beautiful world.

So Saint Luke followed Jesus as His disciple.

He was very close to Saint Paul and travelled with him. He was a clever writer. So he wrote down all that the Apostles did.

This book we call the Acts of the Apostles.

Then he went to see Our Lady. He asked her all about the Baby Jesus. He wrote what she told him in the Gospel According to Saint Luke.

He asked the other Apostles what they knew about Jesus, and their stories are told in his Gospel.

He travelled with Saint Paul all over the world.

He told people that although he could heal their bodies, only Jesus could heal their souls.

He painted a lovely picture of the Blessed Virgin.

We still have copies of it.

In the end, the pagans of Greece killed him because they hated Jesus.

His Feast is October 18th.

St. Martin Of Tours
THE GOOD SOLDIER

The father and mother of Martin did not believe in God.

So when Martin wanted to become a Christian, they wouldn't let him. Instead, his father put him into the army when he was only fifteen.

Martin was a good soldier. Though most of the soldiers were not Christians, he loved Our Lord.

One winter night, Martin met a poor beggar, freezing in the snow. Martin had no money, so he took his sword, cut his cloak in half and gave one half to the beggar.

That night, Our Lord came to him wearing the half cloak. He heard Jesus say to the angels,

"Look; though Martin is not yet baptized, he gave Me his garment."

So Martin became a Christian and converted his parents too.

Because he was brave and strong, the people asked him to stop being a soldier and become their bishop. He did. He is one of the great apostles of France.

His traditional Feast is November 12th.

St. Matthew

GOSPEL WRITER

Once upon a time there was a tax gatherer named Levi.

The Jews did not like him. He took their tax money and gave it to the Romans. But Levi was not a bad man. He only did what he thought was his duty.

One day Jesus saw him. He saw good in him that others did not see. "Come and follow Me!" Jesus said quietly to the tax gatherer.

Levi looked up in surprise. He had never seen such a wonderful Man before. Why, it would be the greatest honor to be one of His followers!

Instantly he got up. He left his table with all the money on it. He went after our Lord. And Jesus made him one of His twelve Apostles.

He changed his name to Matthew. He wrote the wonderful Gospel According to Saint Matthew.

He saw all that Jesus did. He heard all that Jesus said. He walked with Him and grew to love Him more and more.

To make sure that the world would never forget Jesus, Matthew wrote all this down in his beautiful Gospel. Gospel, you know, means Good News.

He died a blessed martyr.

With Saint Mark, Saint Luke and Saint John, he is one of the Four Evangelists.

His Feast is September 21st.

St. Michael

WARRIOR & ARCHANGEL

Saint Michael is one of the Archangels. He is a warrior of God.

Once upon a time long ago, the bad angels made war in Heaven. They cried, "We will not serve!" They raised the red flag. They tried to drive God from the Heavenly City.

But Michael led the armies of the good angels. He drove out the evil army. He knelt before God and cried that God was his only King.

So God made him the General of His armies.

All through history, Michael has fought the battle of God.

He is the Devil's strong enemy. He is the friend and protector of all those who love God and follow Jesus Christ.

He protected the Chosen People, the Jews, in their wars against their enemies. He is always on the side that is right and good.

In the end of the world, a bad man named Antichrist will come. He will make war on Christ and the good people. But Michael and his army will drive him from the world.

That is why we pray after Mass, "Saint Michael, the Archangel, defend us in the day of battle."

His Feast is September 29th.

St. Patrick

Patrick's name was a very noble one. It was taken from a Latin name that meant "a nobleman."

Everyone loves Patrick, so many countries say he was born there. But wherever he was born, he became the friend of all and the Apostle of Ireland.

The Irish in those days did not know about Jesus and Mary. Patrick felt very sorry for them.

He studied hard, and became a priest and a bishop.

The Pope sent him to Ireland to make it Catholic. The people of Ireland welcomed him with joy. The kings sat and listened to him. All the soldiers and colleens asked to be baptized.

He taught them about the Blessed Trinity by showing them how the shamrock had three leaves yet was one plant.

He drove all evils out of Ireland as if they were snakes.

Soon he built churches and schools everywhere. And Saint Brigid worked for the women while Saint Patrick worked for the men.

Since Saint Patrick's time, the Irish have carried the love of Jesus and Mary all over the world. That's why everyone loves Saint Patrick and keeps his feast day.

His Feast is March 17th.

St. Paul
THE COMMUNICATOR

At first his name was Saul. He hated Jesus Christ and all who believed in Him.

He helped the men who killed Saint Stephen, the first martyr.

Next he got an order from the judges to arrest Christians everywhere and put them to death.

But as he rode away to do this, a light struck him from his horse. The voice of Jesus called him. Saul was deeply sorry. He believed in Jesus Christ. He became one of His greatest Apostles.

He travelled on land and sea to tell people about Our Lord. He taught the simple. He talked to the learned. He was shipwrecked. He was thrown into prison. But nothing stopped him from preaching Christ and His Cross.

Thousands believed in Jesus because of this great man. God changed his name to Paul. He wrote beautiful letters called Epistles.

In the end, he was killed with Saint Peter in Rome.

Saint Peter and Paul are both buried in the great Church of Saint Peter.

His traditional Feast is June 30th.

St. Peter
THE ROCK & FIRST POPE

Simon was a fine fisherman when Jesus called him to be an Apostle. "I will make you a fisher of men," said Jesus.

Later he became the Rock, for he was brave and strong. But often he boasted and ran into temptation.

Our Lord made him His special friend. He explained everything important to him. One night, He even let Simon walk on the water. But when Simon grew afraid, Our Lord had to rescue him.

Then one day, Simon made a great act of faith in Christ. Our Lord changed his name to Peter, which means The Rock. He made him the Head of His Church. Peter was the first pope.

Yet when Our Lord was arrested, Peter was afraid. He told everyone he was not an Apostle.

But when he wept bitterly, Jesus forgave him. He made him chief Shepherd of His flock.

Peter ruled the Church bravely. In the end, he died nailed to a cross, upside down.

His Feast is June 29th.

St. Robert

THE MONK

Robert was a young monk who lived in England.

He heard that a group of holy young men wanted to love God very much. They wanted to be especially good to sinners. So he left his comfortable home and joined them. Soon other brave young men came. Together they built a beautiful monastery.

There the poor could come for food. England had few hotels in those days. So travellers could stay over night in Robert's monastery. He gathered boys and girls to teach them about Jesus. He welcomed the sick and took care of them in his hospital.

He never ate until the poor were fed. He gave away his own clothes. He sat up all night long to care for the sick. Once, as he was sitting at dinner, a friend gave him bread sweetened with honey.

But through the window, he saw a poor man. He picked up the bread and honey, placed it on a plate, and carried it to the poor man.

Next day, as he sat at dinner, the plate appeared in the air. It was bright and shining like gold. Then the monks knew that the poor man to whom Robert had given the bread and honey was Christ Himself.

When Robert died, his soul, like a bright ball of fire, went straight up into heaven. The monks heard God's voice saying, "Enter into heaven!"

His Feast is June 7th.

St. Sebastian

THE ATHLETE-SOLDIER

Sebastian was a captain in the Roman army, a fine officer and a brave soldier.

One day he heard about Jesus Christ and said, "He is the one I want to follow." So from that day he loved Christ and fought bravely for Him.

One day his two brothers were arrested. "You are Christians, and you must die," said the judge.

They were only boys, and they were afraid. But Sebastian comforted them, saying, "Don't be afraid. We shall all be martyrs. It is glorious to die for Christ."

The Mayor of Rome did not believe in Jesus Christ. He heard about Sebastian and sent for the young soldier. "Tell me about Jesus," he ordered. And Sebastian talked so beautifully that the Mayor became a Christian too. This made the people who hated Jesus very angry. They began to kill the Christians.

Many of the Christians fled from Rome. Although Sebastian helped them escape he refused to leave.

So the Romans arrested Sebastian. They tied him to a stake. Soldiers shot at him with bows and arrows.

They left him for dead. But Sebastian was not dead. He was still alive and he went to the judge who had ordered him shot. "Please believe in Jesus," he begged. But instead they beat him to death with clubs.

His traditional Feast is January 20th.

St. Stephen
THE FIRST MARTYR

Stephen loved Jesus very much. He worked hard for the poor. He told everyone that Christ was their Savior.

So many people followed him. They listened while he spoke. For his eyes were bright with love for Jesus. And he spoke beautifully of what Jesus had taught and done.

One day the enemies of Jesus said, "We must stop this man. We killed Jesus. But this Stephen still makes others believe in Jesus. We must kill him too."

First they ordered him to stop preaching. He laughed. He could not stop talking about the Savior he loved. So they caught him. They dragged him outside the city.

He stood facing them, this fine young man.

He loved them because Jesus had died for their sakes. He hoped he could make them all Christians.

So he told them about Jesus. He reminded them that Jesus was the very Savior they had hoped to see. He told them that Jesus was not dead but had ascended into heaven.

Angrily, they picked up rocks. They flung them at Stephen. He fell dead. But first he saw Jesus coming to take him.

He was the first martyr.

His Feast is December 26th.

St. Thomas Aquinas
THE SCHOLAR

Thomas Aquinas was a Dominican priest.

His family did not want him to be a priest. They tried very hard to stop him. But he longed to say mass and preach. In the end, he won.

Thomas became a great student. He learned to know all about Our Lord and His teachings. Young people came from all over the world to listen to his classes.

He wrote a wonderful book called the Summa.

Priests and wise men still study it today.

But he also wrote beautiful poetry and hymns. The hymns you sing at Benediction were written by Thomas.

One day Our Lord, hanging on the cross, said to Thomas: "You have written well about Me, Thomas. What reward do you wish?"

"Only yourself," answered the saint.

He knew that if he had Jesus, he had everything.

Millions of people still read the books and sing the hymns of this saint.

The Church calls him the Teacher who was like an Angel.

His Feast is January 28th.

St. Vincent de Paul

THE ORPHAN SAINT

Vincent de Paul was a very holy priest.
He remembered how Our Lord loved the poor and worked for them. So he did all he could to make life sweet and easy for them.

He gave them whatever money he had. He carried the poor sick home and took care of them in his own house. When he found poor children, he gave them food, clothing, toys, and his love.

But always he told them about Jesus Christ. He told them that the Savior was poor too, and loved the poor most of all. Once he was captured by pirates and carried away to sea.

But he made the pirate himself love Jesus Christ and became a Catholic.

To help him work for the poor, he gathered fine men and women about him. They continued his work after he died.

The men are called Priests of the Mission.

The women are the Sisters of Charity who do so much for the poor.

His traditional Feast is July 19th.

INDEX

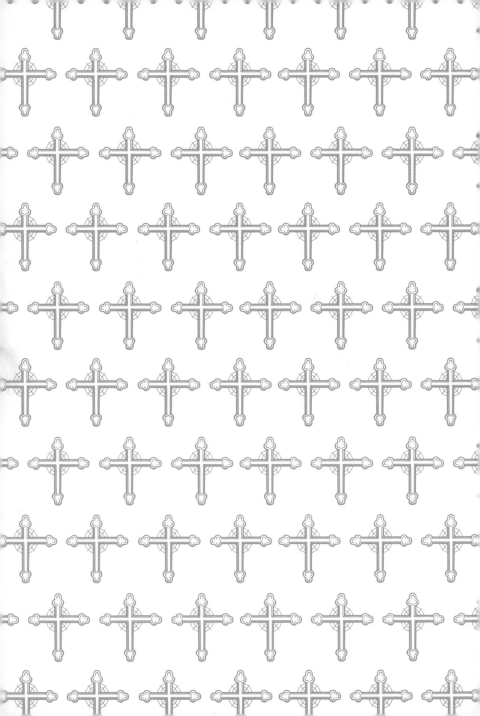